Tyne to Titanic

The Story of Rescue Ship Carpathia

'O hear us when we cry to thee
For those in peril on the sea.'

Ken Smith

Newcastle Libraries & Information Service

The author would like to thank the staff of Tyne & Wear Archives for their help in tracing photographs, the staff of Newcastle Libraries & Information Service for their enthusiastic assistance, staff of the University of Liverpool Library, and Merseyside Maritime Museum, for their help, and particularly the Illustrated London News Picture Library for their generous permission to use so many illustrations.

The author would also like to thank the editor of the *Northumberland Gazette* for kind permission to use quotations from an article in the *Alnwick Gazette*, 1912.

Illustrations acknowledgements:

Swan Hunter Records at Tyne & Wear Archives: 4, 5, 7, 9, 10, 12;
Illustrated London News Picture Library: front and back cover, 6, 14, 15, 18, 22, 23, 24, 26, 28;
The Board of Trustees National Museums and Galleries on Merseyside: 17;
The University of Liverpool Library: 20.

Text © Ken Smith, 1998

ISBN: 1 85795 024 0

British Library Cataloguing in Publication data: a catalogue record for this book is available from the British Library.

Printed by Bailes the Printer, Houghton le Spring

Front cover: A *Titanic* lifeboat approaches the *Carpathia* on the morning of April 15th 1912.

Back cover: Women passengers aboard *Carpathia* sewing and distributing clothes to survivors.

Both photographs reproduced courtesy of the Illustrated London News Picture Library.

Other books by Ken Smith published by Newcastle Libraries & Information Service:

Mauretania: Pride of the Tyne, Newcastle Libraries & Information Service, with Tyne & Wear Museums, 1997.

Turbinia: the Story of Charles Parsons and his Ocean Greyhound, Newcastle Libraries & Information Service with Tyne & Wear Museums, 1996.

A free catalogue and further information is available from

Publications
City Library
Princess Square
Newcastle upon Tyne
NE99 1DX

Contents

Illustrations

Carpathia on the stocks at C.S. Swan and Hunter's Wallsend Shipyard prior to her launch, 1902.

~Birth of a Liner~

On the morning of April 15 1912 the Tyne-built liner *Carpathia* rescued the bitterly cold and traumatised survivors of the *Titanic* disaster. She had been 58 miles away from the sinking ship when she picked up her distress call and she immediately responded by steaming into the night at full speed towards the *Titanic*'s reported position.

Carpathia braved numerous icebergs in the hope of reaching the stricken ship before she slipped beneath the surface of the Atlantic. However, when she arrived at the disaster scene there was no sign of the great White Star liner which many had thought unsinkable. The *Titanic* had disappeared into the depths well over an hour previously with the loss of more than 1,500 lives.

But the *Carpathia* picked up the 705 *Titanic* passengers and crew who had managed to board the ship's lifeboats. To the survivors she must have seemed like a miracle as she steamed out of the dawn. *Carpathia*'s signal rockets had sparkled fitfully in the moonless night and then, as she drew closer, her porthole and mast lights had shone out like beacons of hope amid the gathering light. She was indeed a ship of hope, a liner of mercy bringing warmth and humanity out of a cruelly cold dawn.

Carpathia's birth on the River Tyne had been accompanied, like so many births, by emotions of pride and happiness. It was on April 24th 1903 that the passenger cargo liner departed her fitting out quay at the Wallsend Shipyard of C.S. Swan and Hunter Ltd. Proud yard workers who had built her stood on

*A bow view of **Carpathia** in dry dock, showing her impressive lines. The tall single funnel was painted in the famous Cunard red and black colours.*

75 FEET FROM BOAT DECK TO WATER.

An artist's impression of **Titanic** *in the throes of disaster from the* **Illustrated London News**.

Titanic *had been going too fast in view of the ice warnings and the ship lacked sufficient lifeboats to accommodate all those on board. In addition, her lookouts and officers did not have binoculars – these had been left behind in Southhampton – and the design of the liner's watertight compartments was fatally flawed. More recently, it has been suggested that the ship's steel plating and rivets were of unsatisfactory quality. Not all the lifeboats lowered from the* **Titanic** *were full.*

*An entrance lobby, showing a fine staircase. The ship's name can be seen on **Carpathia**'s floor covering.*

the quay and cheered loudly as she began moving slowly down the River Tyne for preliminary trials in the North Sea and delivery to her owners, Cunard in Liverpool.

It was a thrilling moment for them to see the finished result of their labours and craftsmanship – she was yet another ship proving to the world the high standards achieved by the Tyne's workmen and naval architects.

Carpathia's keel had been laid down at Wallsend on September 10th 1901 and she was launched just under a year later, on August 6th 1902. During the building of the liner excavations in the yard had uncovered the eastern end of Hadrian's Wall.

The ship's completion was delayed by a joiners' strike – her interiors contained a great deal of woodwork as was usual in liners of her era – but the day had at last arrived for her to begin a career upon the sea.

The 558ft-long vessel, bearing one tall funnel painted in Cunard's red and black livery, was 13,555 gross tons, making her one of the company's intermediate-sized liners. She was equipped with two quadruple expansion engines built by the Wallsend Slipway and Engineering Company Ltd, whose works were situated at Willington Quay, only a short distance down river from the shipyard. The engines were linked to two propellers which gave her a top speed of around 15 knots.

Carpathia was not a sumptuous luxury liner – she was built to carry second- and third-class passengers. But the ship provided, for relatively cheap fares, a superior standard of accommodation for such travellers than previously offered.

At the date of her completion she could take over 200 passengers in 2nd class and more than 1,500 in third. Nearly 500 third-class (steerage) passengers were provided with cabins, including two, four and six-berth. But the majority in steerage were accommodated in dormitory areas.

The public rooms in third class were indeed of a high standard for her day. They featured a spacious wood-panelled dining saloon with revolving chairs to seat 300, a large

smoking room, a ladies' sitting room, a bar and covered promenade. The second-class public rooms included a dining saloon to seat 200, a spacious ladies' room and library, and a gentlemen's smoking room.

Besides passengers, the liner was equipped to carry chilled beef from the United States in refrigerated compartments. Three large refrigerating engines were fitted on the upper deck forward for this purpose. Another, smaller refrigerating engine was installed for the ship's provisions. In addition, *Carpathia* had 14 steam winches and 18 cargo derricks to enable speedy loading and discharging of cargo. Among the most important items she carried were the mails to and from America, earning her the title Royal Mail Steamship (RMS) *Carpathia*.

After several successful trial runs over the measured mile, during which *Carpathia* exceeded her guaranteed speed, the ship prepared for her delivery voyage under the command of Captain Barr.

Shipyard men and other visitors who had joined the vessel for the trials but who were not staying for the voyage now boarded a paddle tug. A lively sea buffeted the tug, which pitched and rolled. The bravest visitors jumped for the paddle box, while others strongly gripped the Jacob's ladder and were helped aboard by crewmen.

The tug then steamed away towards the mouth of the Tyne and those aboard her cheered as they waved farewell with their hats to the people lining *Carpathia*'s decks. Then the Cunard liner turned northwards, steaming through the coastal waters of Northumberland as dusk fell.

Passengers looking from portholes or taking an early stroll on deck the next morning could see the Scottish fishing port of Peterhead abeam, its red granite buildings standing out against a background of distant mountains and hills.

Carpathia forged onwards, reaching the coast of Caithness, where passengers briefly sighted the town of Wick. Passing Ducansby Head on the extreme north-east coast of Scotland, she then entered the Pentland Firth between Caithness and the

Plain but sturdy. A section of the third-class dining saloon. **Carpathia** *carried many emigrants in third class from the Mediterranean to America.*

A stern view of the rescue ship in dry dock at Liverpool. Note her two propellers and four masts. Equipped with 18 derricks, she carried refrigerated meat cargoes and mail as well as passengers.

Orkneys. Passengers gained a good view of the Pentland Skerries amid fine weather.

After she left the firth she encountered for the first time the swell of the North Atlantic, an ocean with which she would soon be well acquainted. By the evening the ship was steaming past the high cliffs of Cape Wrath, the most north-westerly point of the British mainland. She then lay at anchor in the North Minch for several hours during the night because of the difficulties involved in passing through this stretch of water into the Little Minch.

The next morning *Carpathia* entered the Little Minch between North Uist and Skye. Among those aboard were directors of the shipbuilders, C.S. Swan and Hunter, including the chairman, George B. Hunter, and Charles Sheriton Swan, junior, son of the company's founder. Also present was Wallsend Yard manager Christopher Stephenson, yard naval architect E.W. De Rusett and the manager of the Wallsend Slipway and Engineering Co Ltd., Andrew Laing.

They and officials of the Cunard Line carried out a thorough inspection of the vessel and found everything in order. The Tyne's shipbuilders and engineers were leaving nothing to chance. The reputation of the river's work was at stake. Orders depended on getting everything exactly right.

Passengers gazed at the beautiful coasts and landscapes of the Hebrides. Others took part in games on deck, including a tug-of-war and an egg-and-spoon race. Dinner that evening was followed by speeches and music in celebration of the anticipated arrival at Liverpool.

Early next morning *Carpathia* passed the Mull of Kintyre and entered the North Channel. Soon she was heading into the Irish Sea, passing the Isle of Man, and then she steamed towards the Mersey. Blackpool Tower was abeam as breakfast was served. The wonderful trip was nearly over. Ship and engine builders would soon be on their way back to Tyneside by train.

At the entrance to the Mersey the Cunard tender *Skirmisher* came alongside to embark the guests who were landed safely in Liverpool after a successful passage.

Carpathia was now poised for her first voyage across the Atlantic, bound for the shores of the New World with hopeful emigrants seeking a better life. It was a challenge for any new ship and her crew. But the liner's greatest challenge still lay nine years ahead, a challenge which would bring her to the attention of the world. Then the name of the liner from the Tyne would be on everyone's lips.

TRAGEDY OF THE ATLANTIC.

The Titanic Disaster : Appalling Death Roll.

Nearly Fifteen Hundred Lives Lost

868 SURVIVORS ON BOARD THE CARPATHIA.

ROYAL MESSAGES OF SYMPATHY.

From the **Newcastle Daily Journal** *April 1912. The number of survivors on board* **Carpathia**, *and the death toll, was not accurately known at this time.*

Carpathia at sea. She served on the New York-Trieste, Liverpool-New York and Liverpool-Boston routes. At the time she picked up the **Titanic**'s distress call she was on her way to the Mediterranean, bound for Gibraltar and ultimately Trieste. The rescue ship was 58 miles to the south-east of the sinking liner.

~Maiden Voyage~

Carpathia sailed on her maiden voyage from Liverpool bound for Boston on May 5th 1903. The Cunard tender brought over 1,000 third-class passengers to her at 11am. They had come from almost every country in Europe. Then, at 3pm, *Carpathia* came alongside the landing stage to embark the second-class passengers and their luggage.

Within just over an hour all was ready. Visitors were ordered ashore and the gangway lifted. A crowd waved farewell on the quayside as the ship moved slowly away at 4.15pm.

The Irish Sea was uncharacteristically calm with virtually no wind as *Carpathia* steamed onwards. The weather remained placid throughout the night. The next morning the ship was off the coast of Waterford with a large number of fishing boats in sight.

It was gone 10am when *Carpathia* entered Queenstown Harbour in County Cork to embark the Irish passengers. These were brought to the ship by a tender. As each person came aboard holding their ticket to America they were checked by a doctor and then guided by stewards to their quarters.

Cunard agents from Queenstown and members of the Press also boarded to inspect the vessel. While they looked around, other visitors were plying their trade. These were a group of hawkers and street traders who sold items such as Irish laces, shawls, and souvenirs made of bog-oak. The Irish newspapers were also on sale.

At 12.30pm it was time for the hawkers and other visitors to depart in the tender and *Carpathia* steamed out of Queenstown Harbour towards the Old Head of Kinsale. Later she passed Cape Clear and finally the Fastness Rock, that last outpost of Ireland before the open Atlantic.

In the morning there was talk of a new passenger joining the ship. Some were puzzled, but soon it became clear that one of the Irish emigrant women had given birth to a son. A baby of the Atlantic, it was not long before he was dubbed 'Carpathius' by some of the passengers.

The next morning, May 8th, a heavy sea developed with squalls amid a strong northerly breeze. The ship rolled but few regarded it as rough. By May 11 the breeze had moderated.

The better weather brought passengers on to the open deck for a stroll. Others played games including cricket, a form of bowls and curling combined, deck quoits, shuffle-board, ping-pong and deck golf. Chess, draughts, dominoes and whist kept other passengers amused in the smoking rooms.

The sea became smoother as *Carpathia* reached the Grand Banks off Newfoundland and whales and porpoises delighted eager watchers on deck.

At 11am on May 14 the ship docked safely in Boston Harbour after passing numerous schooners, yachts and other steamships. The outward passage of 3,009 miles had been covered at an average speed of 14.9 knots. It had lasted a few hours under nine days.

The *Carpathia*'s cargo and mails were unloaded and a new cargo, of beef, was taken aboard into the refrigerated holds. The work went on throughout the night.

On May 17 the liner departed Boston on the return leg of her voyage. She disembarked Irish passengers and unloaded mail at Queenstown on May 25, and arrived in Liverpool the following day. The homeward passage had been accomplished at an average speed of 15.1 knots. Her best run had been to cover 383 miles in one day. The liner's engines had performd well and Cunard must have been pleased with their new ship from Wallsend.

Carpathia was later switched to the Liverpool-New York run and appears to have had a relatively uneventful but successful career on this route. Then, in the autumn of 1903, came another change. She was transferred to the Trieste-New York route, carrying mainly Hungarian and Italian emigrants. Calls were made at Fiume (now Rijeka), Palermo, Naples, Genoa and Gibraltar. The next year, however, saw the ship back on the Liverpool-New York run.

In 1905 *Carpathia*'s accommodation was changed so that she could now carry 100 first-class passengers, 200 second and over 2,000 in third. She then returned to the Trieste-New York route, again picking up emigrants bound for America, but also taking comfortably-off US tourists on pleasure trips to the Mediterranean. The ship was to stay on this service until after the outbreak of the First World War in 1914.

The wireless room or 'shack' of an early 20th century liner. The operator sits with headphones on, taking down the mesages he hears in morse code from other ships. **Carpathia***'s operator, Harold Cottam, would have worked in similar conditions. Twenty-four hour radio cover was not provided because he was the only 'Marconi man' aboard. Only the largest ships carried two operators in those days. The wireless operator of the cargo steamer* **Californian** *missed the Titanic's distress call beacause he had gone to bed. By chance,* **Carpathia***'s Cottam was still on duty.*

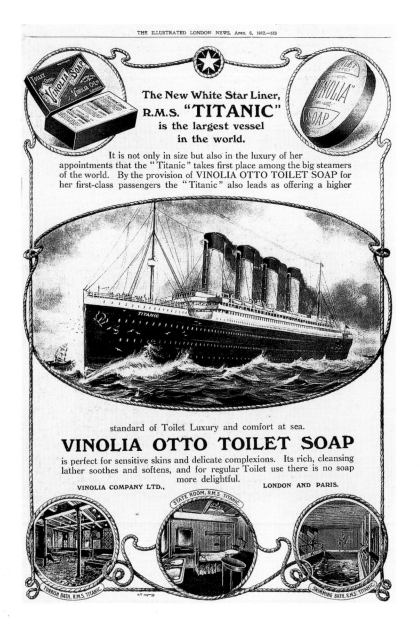

The New White Star Liner,
R.M.S. "TITANIC"
is the largest vessel
in the world.

It is not only in size but also in the luxury of her appointments that the "Titanic" takes first place among the big steamers of the world. By the provision of VINOLIA OTTO TOILET SOAP for her first-class passengers the "Titanic" also leads as offering a higher standard of Toilet Luxury and comfort at sea.

VINOLIA OTTO TOILET SOAP

is perfect for sensitive skins and delicate complexions. Its rich, cleansing lather soothes and softens, and for regular Toilet use there is no soap more delightful.

VINOLIA COMPANY LTD.,   LONDON AND PARIS.

TURKISH BATH, R.M.S. TITANIC.   STATE ROOM, R.M.S. TITANIC.   SWIMMING BATH, R.M.S. TITANIC.

*An advertisement from the **Illustrated London News**, April 6th 1912. The soap company was obviously proud to be associated with the prestigious new ship. Less than two weeks after this advertisement appeared the **Titanic** was at the bottom of the ocean.*

*Wealthy **Titanic** passengers. Top right and left, millionaire John Jacob Astor and his young wife Madeleine, who were returning from a holiday in Europe and Egypt when disaster struck. Madeleine, aged 19, was seven months pregnant. By the time she was picked up by the **Carpathia** she was a widow.*

Below, Benjamin Guggenheim, of the American mining empire family. He remained on board the sinking ship and calmly faced the end with his valet. They are reported to have worn full evening dress and to have lit cigars as the tilt of the decks grew ever steeper.

~Dash to the Rescue~

There is an unwritten code among seamen, whether they be enemies in war or rivals in peace – to go to the aid of other mariners in distress. Captain Arthur Rostron, master of the *Carpathia*, could not have been aware when his ship departed New York on April 11 1912 that he would soon be called upon to follow this law of the oceans in a humanitarian mission of epic proportions.

Captain Rostron, who was born in Bolton, Lancashire, had been an officer with Cunard since 1895 and was given command of *Carpathia* in January 1912 at the age of 42.

This was the sixth ship he had commanded for the line and as she pulled away from Pier 54 Rostron had every reason to be proud of his record. Judging by his subsequent actions it is clear that he was a man of rapid decisiveness and practical attention to detail. These qualities were combined with compassion, humanity and a great ability to get his crew to respond to their utmost, rapidly and efficiently. He was aptly nicknamed the 'Electric Spark'.

Captain Rostron was a seaman of the old school – he had served in sail during his younger days. Conscientious, he set high standards for himself and all around him in keeping with the proud traditions of his watery profession. 'Seamanlike' is an old term that might best describe his qualities. Strict in many ways with his crew, he nevertheless displayed a gentle reserve, together with a concern for his fellow human beings. Religious, he was a believer in the power of prayer.

As his ship cleared New York harbour early on the afternoon of April 11, another vessel on the other side of the Atlantic was departing from her anchorage off Queenstown, while on her maiden voyage, a voyage she would never

complete. This 46,300-ton liner, the biggest in the world at that date, was a four-funnel White Star ship carrying more than 2,200 passengers and crew. She bore a name destined to echo down the many years which have elapsed since. That one word – *Titanic* – remains indelibly printed on the face of 20th century history. Her maiden voyage was taking place amid a blaze of publicity with some people claiming that she was virtually unsinkable.

By the night of April 14th *Carpathia* was well on course for Gibraltar and about 1,000 miles east of New York. The weather had turned bitterly cold but the sky was wonderfully clear with many stars and the lights of the Aurora Borealis visible.

The ship's young wireless operator, Harold Cottam, had been on duty since the early morning. Only the biggest and most prestigious liners carried two operators in those early days of radio communication and so Cottam had to work long hours. Throughout the day and evening he was busy relaying wireless messages (then known as Marconigrams) to and from passengers as well as other ships. He knew the *Titanic* was not far away. She was within the range of *Carpathia*'s wireless and Cottam heard her operators transmitting messages to the Cape Race station in the United States.

Another feature of his day had been a series of ice warnings from other ships. The first was from the Cunard passenger liner *Caronia* which reported sighting ice to the north of *Carpathia*. Later, reports of an icefield in the same area came from the White Star passenger liner *Baltic* and from the cargo steamers *Californian* and *Messaba*. These warnings were heard by the *Titanic*.

The industrious Cottam passed the messages to the bridge

*Disaster ship. The **Titanic**, which sank at 2.20 am on April 15 1912 after striking an iceberg on her maiden voyage. More than 1,500 lives were lost. This photograph shows **Titanic** leaving Southampton. She called at Cherbourg and Queenstown before setting out on her passage to tragedy.*

*The man who picked up the distress call. Harold Cottam, wireless operator of the **Carpathia**, pictured in the Illustrated London News. He had been about to go to bed when he heard the message.*

"Illustrated London News"

and from them Rostron and his officers were able to calculate that *Carpathia* was well clear of the icefield to the north. Rostron surveyed the scene and could see no bergs or growlers (smaller blocks of ice) but the captain ordered that a sharp lookout be kept.

By just after midnight, Cottam was extremely tired and he began preparing to turn into bed for the night. However, the enthusiastic young operator kept his earphones on as he began unlacing his boots. Cottam called the *Titanic* to tell them there was a batch of messages on the airwaves for the ship. It was then that *Titanic*'s operator butted in with an extraordinary message. He asked the *Carpathia* to 'come at once' and added: 'We have struck an iceberg'. The operator gave *Titanic*'s position as Latitude 41.46 North, Longitude 50.14 West. He confirmed to Cottam they required immediate assistance.

Carpathia's stunned radio man raced from his wireless 'shack' to the bridge and told the officer on watch that *Titanic* had sent out a distress call. They then went to Rostron's cabin. The captain was trying to get to sleep and was annoyed by their sudden entrance.

For a few seconds, he found the news that *Titanic* had hit a berg and was sinking difficult to believe. Could such a disaster really be happening to this great ship on her maiden voyage? He asked Cottam if he was absolutely certain the message was correct. The operator was adamant. *Titanic* had sent out the old distress call, CQD, and the new one, SOS.

The captain's doubts were ended. He went to the chart room where he worked out that the stricken liner's reported position was 58 miles to the north-west of *Carpathia*. Rostron sprang into immediate action. He ordered the ship to be turned around. *Carpathia* began moving on a north-westerly bearing as she worked up to full steam. She was now sailing in the opposite direction to Gibraltar, towards an icefield.

Rostron showed his efficiency and humanity as he meticulously prepared his ship for her rescue mission. Those members of the crew not on duty were roused from their sleep and the officers were assembled to be briefed by the captain on the tasks required.

He instructed that every member of the crew be served coffee to fortify them for the difficulties and hard work ahead.

The measures taken were almost military in their thoroughness and attention to detail. The lifeboats were swung out in readiness to pick up survivors and canvas ash bags were brought out so that small children could be brought aboard in them if necessary. Bosun's chairs were also made ready to lift other survivors. Gangway doors were opened and lines prepared for throwing to *Titanic*'s lifeboats.

Ladders were fastened to *Carpathia*'s sides and strong lights sited at the gangways. Rostron even ordered that chairs be brought on deck together with ropes to bind any survivors who might become hysterical as a result of their ordeal.

In addition, he told the stewards to have blankets, soup, tea, coffee and brandy ready. The two dining saloons became first aid stations and the ship's three doctors (British, Hungarian and Italian) were posted to them.

Rostron was determined that *Carpathia* would be in a high state of readiness by the time she reached the disaster area. But could she reach the *Titanic* before she sank? The question must have plagued him continually as his ship raced through the early hours on a glass-like sea.

The captain did what he could to ensure the vessel's engines achieved their maximum potential. Her hot water was shut off so that all available heat could be turned into steam and extra stokers were employed keeping the furnaces fed. It is likely *Carpathia* achieved a speed of between 15 and 16 knots during the next few hours. Later, it would be claimed that she had reached 17 knots or more but this would not have been possible for her engines. However, it is beyond doubt that her Wallsend-built engines served her well.

Whatever her speed, Rostron must have been acutely aware of the risks ahead as he began the dash to the north-west in search of the ill-fated *Titanic*. His ship was carrying more than 700 passengers and she was sailing at full steam during the night into waters where an icefield had been reported. It was a dangerous situation and great care had to be taken with the helm. The lives of *Carpathia*'s passengers as well as *Titanic*'s survivors were at stake.

Accordingly, extra seamen were posted to keep lookout and it was not long before the need for such action was confirmed. *Carpathia* began encountering a series of bergs and altered course to avoid them. A sharp lookout by officers and men proved effective and on at least one occasion a berg was spotted by star-shine reflected from its surface. Meanwhile, Cottam had radioed to the *Titanic* that *Carpathia* was coming to their rescue as fast as she could.

The captain told his crew to go about their tasks as quietly as possible, but passengers began stirring in their cabins and a few made their way on to the open deck as the noise of intense activity aboard awoke them. Initially, some thought *Carpathia* herself was in trouble and many were incredulous when they heard she was going to the rescue of the prestigious new White Star liner, the largest such ship in the world and billed by some as practically unsinkable.

At 2.40 am a green flare was sighted from the bridge. It was a long way ahead but it sent a signal to *Carpathia* that human life was still active in the area of *Titanic*'s last reported position. In reply, at 3am *Carpathia* began firing rockets at 15-minute intervals. These would tell of the rescue ship's approach, giving hope to any survivors.

Carpathia stewards, stewardesses, kitchen staff and other crew members pose for a picture in the aftermath of the rescue. Blankets, tea, coffee, soup and clothing were provided for survivors. Brandy was also available. Many passengers gave up their berths to **Titanic**'s people.

~Lifeboats and Widows~

The ship continued to weave her way through the icefield, with the eyes of lookouts strained towards the horizon. But as they approached the disaster area there was no sign of the *Titanic*, though more green flares were sighted. Rostron must have known then that he was too late.

By 3.30am *Carpathia* found herself in the midst of countless bergs and growlers and Rostron ordered the engines to be put on half speed ahead. By about 4am the ship reached *Titanic's* position and speed had been reduced to slow. They had taken about three-and-a-half hours to get there.

Suddenly, a green flare shone out. It was almost at sea level. Then, as the first light of dawn streamed across the water, Rostron and his men could just make out a lifeboat being rowed with difficulty towards *Carpathia*. All its occupants were exhausted, cold and numbed by their ordeal.

The boat contained 25 women, ten children and five men. Four of the men were at the oars, rowing in a way which betrayed their fatigue. At the tiller was a young ship's officer.

As the boat reached *Carpathia's* side, an officer and two seamen descended rope ladders and boarded her. She was then manoeuvred towards an open doorway and made fast with lines. The women and children were lifted aboard safely in bosun's chairs and canvas ash bags. The five men managed to climb the ladder to the doorway.

As the light grew, Rostron was able to make out other lifeboats scattered over a wide area. There were 20 in all, including four collapsibles. All around them were bergs and growlers which floated like white ghosts on the sea, although more solid than any phantom.

The young *Titanic* officer in the first boat, James Boxhall,
was taken to the bridge where he told Rostron that the *Titanic* had sunk. The great liner foundered at 2.20 am on April 15 1912 with the loss of over 1,500 lives. It must have been difficult for Rostron and his crew to take in. The water in *Carpathia's* vicinity was 33ºF, a mere one degree above freezing point. Anyone in the sea would not have lasted long.

Carpathia's crew continued the task of picking up the survivors. Her own passengers crowded the deck rails, watching the proceedings in stunned silence. Strangely, some of the boats were half empty, but others were packed to capacity with frightened souls chilled as much by their terrible ordeal as by a cold night on the Atlantic. A great number of women survivors were now widows. They searched in vain for their husbands aboard the rescue ship. Children were also without fathers. Out of 11 honeymoon couples on *Titanic*, only one man survived. One woman had become separated from her baby during the evacuation of the *Titanic* but the child safely reached the rescue ship and Rostron was able reunite mother and infant.

The last of the lifeboats to reach *Carpathia's* side was carrying 75 people. It was very low in the water and in danger of being swamped or capsized. The sea was becoming choppy. However, all were embarked safely. The final person to board was *Titanic's* Second Officer, Charles Lightoller, who had taken command of the lifeboat and whose seamanship proved invaluable in keeping it afloat.

Robbie Purvis, from Alnwick, was an 18-year-old steward aboard the rescue ship. He told the *Alnwick Gazette*: 'We came quite close to the iceberg which *Titanic* struck. It was about a mile long and 100 feet high. There were plenty of bergs

*Three survivors from the **Titanic** aboard **Carpathia**. Mr George Harder, who was the only man saved of 11 honeymoon couples, sits with his wife. They are talking to Mrs Charles Hayes, whose husband, president of the Canadian Grand Trunk Railway, was lost. Mrs Hayes was one of the many women made widows by the disaster.*

*Women passengers sewing and distributing clothes to help **Titanic** survivors aboard **Carpathia**. Many had evacuated the sinking liner wearing only light clothing, or had spent some time in the water. **Carpathia** was on course for New York where the survivors were safely landed.*

*Rescue hero. Captain Arthur Rostron with the silver cup presented to him by the grateful **Titanic** survivors. The cup was handed over by first-class passenger Molly Brown from Denver, Colorado.*

He added: 'The *Carpathia* sailed on around the scene of the disaster, the dark, icy water lapping against her iron sides as if mocking her for being too late.'

In all, there were just 705 survivors. Three men died of shock and exposure soon after they were taken aboard.

As the last of the 705 were being picked up at 8.30 am, the cargo ship *Californian* steamed into view from the west. She had been lying stopped amid the ice during the night and her radio operator missed the *Titanic*'s distress call because he had gone to bed. She had now heard the news on the airwaves and asked Rostron if she could be of any help. *Carpathia* became a ship pervaded by a profound sense of loss. Her flags were lowered to half mast and a service in remembrance of the dead and of thanksgiving for those rescued was held in the first-class dining saloon.

The ship steamed slowly around the waters above *Titanic*'s final resting place. Rostron was checking to see if there were any more survivors. But none were seen. Small items of wreckage were visible on the surface, including deck chairs. The *Titanic* now lay more than 13,000 ft below the surface of the Atlantic.

The captain decided to land the survivors at New York and shortly before 9am ordered his ship to steam away from the wreck site to the south-west. They encountered numerous icebergs in their path, some as high as 200ft, but eventually reached clear water after three hours of manoeuvring. They then set course for New York.

The *Californian* had been requested to remain at the disaster scene to check for any possible survivors clinging to wreckage, but Rostron's hopes must have been fading fast. The ship stopped briefly and a funeral service was held for the three men who had died and for a fourth who had passed away in one of the collapsible lifeboats. Their bodies were committed to the deep. The rescue ship's crew and passengers showed great kindness to the survivors and many gave up their cabins for them. Women passengers distributed clothes to survivors,

scattered about, but none so big as this one. We had to come right through amongst them in the dark looking for lifeboats. We sailed exactly over the spot where *Titanic* went down, just a dark patch on the water with deck chairs and cushions and dead bodies (some babies) all floating about amongst the wreckage. It was a heart-rending sight.'

some of whom had evacuated the ship wearing their dressing gowns or light clothing. Those people who had been in the water but who had managed to reach the boats had their wet clothes taken to the ship's ovens for drying.

As *Carpathia* steamed towards the shores of America, radio operator Cottam was deluged with Marconigrams from relatives of *Titanic* passengers and from newspapers seeking the stories of survivors and details of the rescue.

Rostron ordered that no information be divulged to the Press. They would get their stories soon enough, when *Carpathia* docked. But the captain instructed that a list of survivors be transmitted to the Cape Race station. This was sent via the White Star liner *Olympic,* sister ship of the *Titanic.* Cottam was helped in his tasks by *Titanic*'s junior radio operator, Harold Bride, who had been among the rescued. They also transmitted messages to relatives of the survivors, but it was a difficult task because the airwaves were crowded with inquiries.

Among the first-class passengers who lost their lives was John Jacob Astor, millionaire hotel owner, who had been returning to America with his 19-year-old pregnant wife Madeleine after visiting Europe and Egypt. Madeleine was one of the widows picked up by *Carpathia.* Also among the wealthy men lost was Benjamin Guggenheim of the US mining business empire.

Isidor Straus, owner of the Macy's Department Store in New York, and his wife Ida were two other rich Americans who failed to return from that tragic maiden voyage. Ida had decided to remain on board with her husband. They bravely faced the end together as the slope of the great ship's decks grew steeper.

However, a larger proportion of third-class passengers lost their lives than first-class. Only 24 per cent of those travelling in third class were rescued as against 63 per cent in first class.

The crew's survival rate was 23 per cent, almost the same as that of the poorest passengers. Only 210 of them lived to tread the decks of *Carpathia* out of 898.

In all, 1503 people lost their lives in an ocean tragedy which shocked the world. The *Titanic*'s master, Captain Edward Smith honourably went down with his ship. All the liner's engineers also perished, a fate shared by the ship's band, who, it is well attested, kept playing until the very last.

The North-East of England, where *Carpathia* had started her life, did not escape the losses. Among crew members who died was Alfred King, described by the *Newcastle Journal* as 'A promising youth of Nile Street, Gateshead'. He had worked for the ship equipment manufacturers Clarke Chapman of Gateshead, but had always wanted to go to sea. Alfred had been employed as lift boy in first class. Engineer C.F.W. Sidgwick, from Sunderland, was also lost. He was on his way to a new job in Mexico and his wife had been due to follow him at a later date. They were newly married. William T. Stead, a famous campaigning journalist and former editor of the *Northern Echo* at Darlington, was another person on the casualty list. He had been born in Northumberland in 1849.

Lightning punctuated the skies and heavy rain drenched *Carpathia*'s decks as she entered New York Harbour on the evening of April 18th 1912. At The Battery thousands thronged the shore to watch her amid the storm. Lightning forked menacingly above the great city's skyline.

Minutes earlier the rescue ship had been greeted by an armada of small craft hired by newspaper reporters. They shouted through megaphones in an attempt to pick up rescue details from passengers and fired off their flash cameras. Some reporters had managed to get aboard the pilot boat and they then tried to board the ship. Only one succeeded. He was confined to the bridge by Rostron and refused any interviews.

Carpathia berthed at Pier 54, from where she had started out, at 9.30 pm and the survivors were disembarked safely. *Titanic* radio operator Harold Bride was carried ashore exhausted, his feet crushed and frost-bitten. The epic rescue was over.

Above, Harold Bride, one of **Titanic**'s two radio operators, is carried ashore from the rescue ship at New York. His bandaged feet are crushed and frostbitten. The other operator, Jack Phillips, was lost. Bride gallantly assisted **Carpathia**'s wireless man during the voyage to New York despite his condition.

Titanic officers. Top, 2nd Officer Charles Lightoller, the last survivor to board **Carpathia.** Right, 6th Officer James Moody who was lost. He was one of two officers on the bridge when the ship struck the iceberg. Left, 5th Officer Harold Lowe, a survivor. He took his lifeboat back towards people in the water in an effort to save lives. Lowe also transferred survivors to his boat from a collapsible boat which was in danger of sinking.

~Fame and Fate~

Two days later, on April 20th, *Carpathia* again left New York to complete her interrupted voyage to the Mediterranean. By this time she and her crew were world famous. When Rostron returned to New York over a month later he found thousands of letters waiting for him from admirers and well-wishers.

The career of Captain Arthur Rostron never looked back after that momentous night in 1912. A plaque bearing his portrait was put on show in New York's Hall of Fame and he was presented with a US Congressional Medal of Honour. Later, he was to receive the Freedom of the City of New York. Other honours followed, including the Gold Medal of the New York Life Saving Benevolent Association and the Insignia of the French Legion of Honour. Between 1915 and 1926 Rostron commanded the magnificent Tyne-built liner *Mauretania*, which held the Blue Riband for more than 20 years. In 1928 he was knighted, later becoming Commodore of the Cunard Line. Like the rockets he fired from his ship, he had shot to fame in one night of decisive action to save lives. But unlike the lights from those rockets, his fame never faded. The compassionate and efficient captain died in 1940.

The *Titanic* survivors set up a fund and medals were issued to Rostron, his officers and crew commemorating the rescue. They also presented the captain with a silver cup. This token of gratitude was handed over by first-class passenger Molly Brown, a spirited American woman from Denver, Colorado, whose strong and optimistic personality had helped to boost morale during the ordeal. In addition a plaque recalling the rescue was sited aboard the liner.

And what became of *Carpathia*, the Wallsend-built rescue ship which was perhaps more famous than her captain? She continued on the Mediterranean run until 1915 when she was transferred to the New York-Liverpool route to carry vital supplies for Britain's war effort.

It was a German U-boat which eventually ended her career, ironically sending her to rest on the Atlantic seabed like the *Titanic*. *Carpathia* was steaming in convoy from Liverpool to New York on July 17th 1918. The ships were about 120 miles south west of the Fastnet Rock and 170 miles north west of the Bishop Rock. It was early morning. A U-boat began shadowing them. Its captain studied the convoy – there were three lines of ships. In the centre of the middle column a passenger-cargo liner stood out above the rest. She was the *Carpathia*, the largest ship of all and an irresistible target to the commander of *U55*.

It was 9.15 am. Two torpedoes hit the engine room amidships and another struck the vessel's forward section. Three trimmers and two firemen were killed by the first torpedo explosion. The attack also proved fatal to *Carpathia*. Captain William Prothero knew his ship would eventually sink, her injuries were too great, and he ordered everyone to take to the lifeboats. She slipped beneath the waves two-and-a-half hours later.

The 275 survivors were picked up by the minesweeping sloop HMS *Snowdrop* which landed them safely at Liverpool.

The story of the *Carpathia* had ended with a wartime attack, a fate she shared with many other merchant vessels of the First World War. But the Tyne-built liner had won for herself a lasting place in the honours list of humane deeds by ships and men.

~Carpathia Facts and Figures~

Builders: C. S. Swan and Hunter Ltd., Wallsend Shipyard.

Owners: Cunard.

Launched: August 6th 1902.

Completed: April 1903.

Gross Tonnage as built: 13,555 tons.

Length: 558 ft.

Engines: Two quadruple expansion, linked to twin propellers. Built by Wallsend Slipway and Engineering Co. Ltd.

Speed on trials: 14.344 knots.

Maiden Voyage: Departed Liverpool for Boston, USA, on May 5th 1903.

Routes: New York -Trieste, Liverpool-New York, Liverpool-Boston.

Honours: Rescued the *Titanic* survivors on the morning of April 15 1912 and took them safely to New York.

Fate: Sunk by torpedoes from a U-boat on July 17th 1918, with loss of five lives.